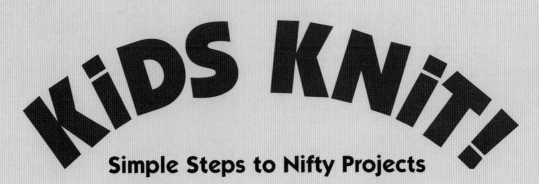

KiDS KNiT!

Simple Steps to Nifty Projects

KIDS KNIT!

Simple Steps to Nifty Projects

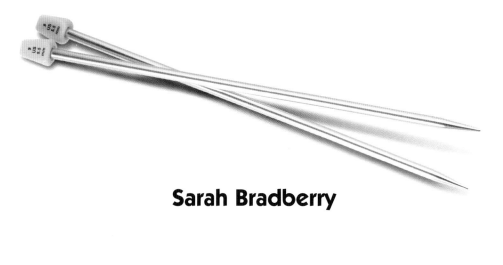

Sarah Bradberry

STERLING PUBLISHING CO., INC.
New York

Editor: *Hazel Chan*

Designer: *Rose Sheifer*

Photos: *Michael Hnatov*

Illustrations: *Kim Coxey*

Special thanks to Martin Viette Nurseries of East Norwich, NY for the use of their location during their fall festival. Photos on pages 2, 4, 6, 8, 10, 16, 20, 27, 28, 35, 40, 45, 69, 70, 72, 73, 78, 82, 83, 91, 96.

Very special thanks to the models in this book: Claire and Hannah (left and right, respectively, on page 1); Jennifer and Emily (left and right, respectively, on page 9); Chandler (on page 16); Max (on page 20).

10 9 8 7 6 5 4 3 2 1

Published by Sterling Publishing Co., Inc.
387 Park Avenue South, New York, NY 10016
© 2004 by Sarah Bradberry
Distributed in Canada by Sterling Publishing
C/o Canadian Manda Group, 165 Dufferin Street
Toronto, Ontario, Canada M6K 3H6
Distributed in Great Britain and Europe by Chris Lloyd at Orca Book
Services, Stanley House, Fleets Lane, Poole BH15 3AJ, England
Distributed in Australia by Capricorn Link (Australia) Pty. Ltd.
P.O. Box 704, Windsor, NSW 2756, Australia

Sterling ISBN 1-4027-2192-7

Contents

What Is Knitting?

Knitting is a way of looping yarn together with two sticks to make a piece of fabric. You can make just about anything with knitting: from wall hangings and blankets, to sweaters and socks, and anything in between!

In the first part of this book, you'll learn about the tools you need to start knitting and a little information about yarn. In the second part, you will learn new knitting skills that will help you make the projects in each chapter. The instructions for the new skills are given before the first project that uses them. This book has twenty projects for you to knit: from dolls to doll blankets, from scarves to backpacks.

If you have trouble with any of the instructions in this book, ask a teacher or relative who knows how to knit to help you. If you don't know anyone who knits, then have an adult take you to a yarn store and ask the owner for help. Many are happy to help their customers, so don't be afraid to ask. Another thing that you can do is to find out if your neighborhood has a knitting guild with meetings that you and your parent can go to. A knitting guild is a group of people who meet regularly to learn new things about knitting, or they can just sit, knit, and have fun. If none of these are available, and you have a computer at home, have an adult help you find knitting websites on the Internet.

Anyone can learn to knit: Boys and girls, kids and adults. So let's get started!

Tools and Yarn

You only need three things to learn how to knit:

1 Yarn.

2 A pair of knitting needles (the right size for your yarn).

3 A pair of scissors to cut your yarn.

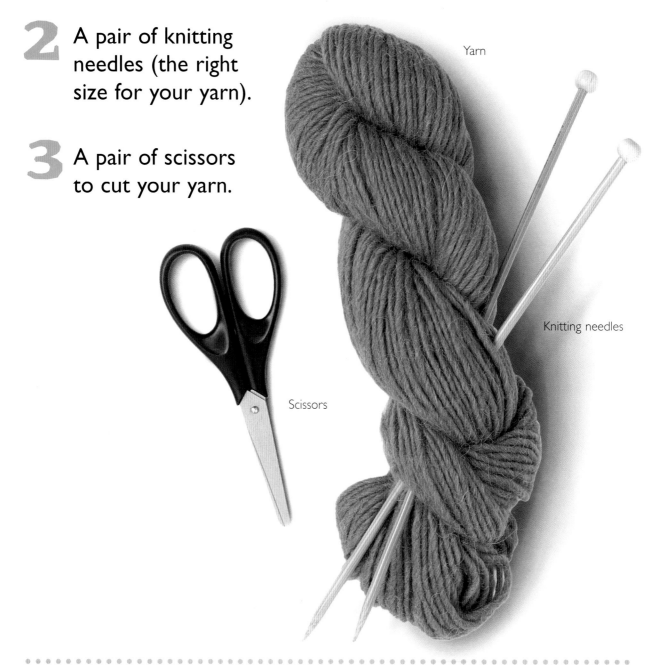

Yarn

Knitting needles

Scissors

When you want to start making things, you'll need a few more **tools**

- A yarn or darning needle for sewing things together.

- A measuring tape to measure you and your knitting.

- Pearl-headed pins to join pieces together while you sew. Do not use ordinary dressmaker's pins. They can get lost in your knitting and accidentally stick you while you are working on your pieces.

- A crochet hook for picking up stitches.

- Safety pins.

- Double-pointed knitting needles.

- A bag to put everything in! You can use a fabric or tote bag, or a thick paper gift bag, for your needles so that they won't poke through. You can also keep your scissors and other small things in a pencil case so they don't get lost or caught up in your knitting.

Pencil case

Safety pins

Measuring tape

Crochet hook

Pearl-headed pins

Yarn needle

Double-pointed needles

Knitting Needles

Knitting needles come in many different shapes and sizes. Some are straight, others are circular. Some are made of metal, others can be made of wood or plastic. But whatever shape and material they come in, knitting needles have a number size. This number tells you how thin or fat the needles are. In the United States, the lower numbers belong to thin needles, the higher numbers belong to fat needles. The size of the needles, plus the thickness of the yarn and how tightly you knit, will affect the size of your finished knitted project.

Each project in this book requires a specific needle size. The number is given in US size. If you live outside of the United States, look at the chart on page 15 to find the same size.

Knitting needles come in many different shapes and sizes

Needle Sizes

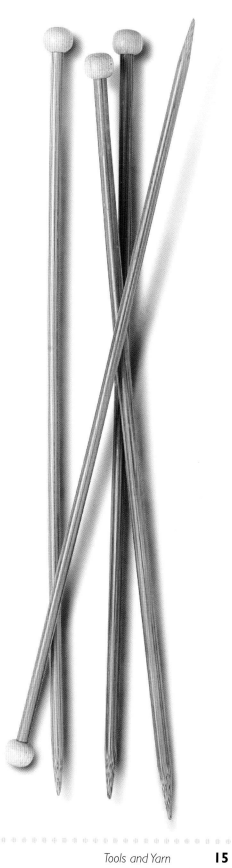

US	Metric	UK
0	2 mm	14
1	2.25 mm	13
	2.5 mm	
2	2.75 mm	12
	3 mm	11
3	3.25 mm	10
4	3.5 mm	
5	3.75 mm	9
6	4 mm	8
7	4.5 mm	7
8	5 mm	6
9	5.5 mm	5
10	6 mm	4
10.5	6.5 mm	3
	7 mm	2
	7.5 mm	1
11	8 mm	0
13	9 mm	00
15	10 mm	000

Yarn

Let's have a quick look at some things you'll need to know (and some things you just might like to know) before you buy your yarn.

Reading Your Yarn Label

When you go into a yarn store and look at different balls of yarn, you will see a lot of numbers and words on the label. Although every label looks different, it should have all the information you need to choose the right yarn for your project.

Your label should have:

- The name of the yarn.
- The thickness of the yarn (see below right).
- How many yards (meters) of yarn are in one ball.

- The weight of the ball of yarn.
- What the yarn is made from (see page 19).
- The color number or name. This is the number or name that the shopkeepers use to tell exactly which color people mean when they ask for their yarn. The people who make the yarn decide what the color number or name is, and everyone calls it the same thing.
- The dyelot number. The dyelot number tells you which balls of yarn were dyed at the same time. If you buy more than one ball of yarn in the same color, make sure they have the same dyelot number. This will tell you that they are from the same batch. If you buy the same color yarn from different dyelots, they may look exactly the same, but they'll probably be slightly different. If you knit them next to each other, they can make a noticeable stripe.
- Washing and drying instructions.
- Suggested gauge. Gauge (sounds like "cage") tells you how big your stitches should be by telling you how many stitches and rows fit in a certain number of inches (centimeters). We'll learn all about gauge when we make the first project in this book (see page 31).

How Thick Is Your Yarn?

The most important thing you need to know when you want to knit something is how thick your yarn is. Different thicknesses have their own names. Starting from the thinnest to thickest, the five most common thicknesses of yarn are: lace weight, fingering, sport weight (also known as double knit weight), worsted weight, and bulky.

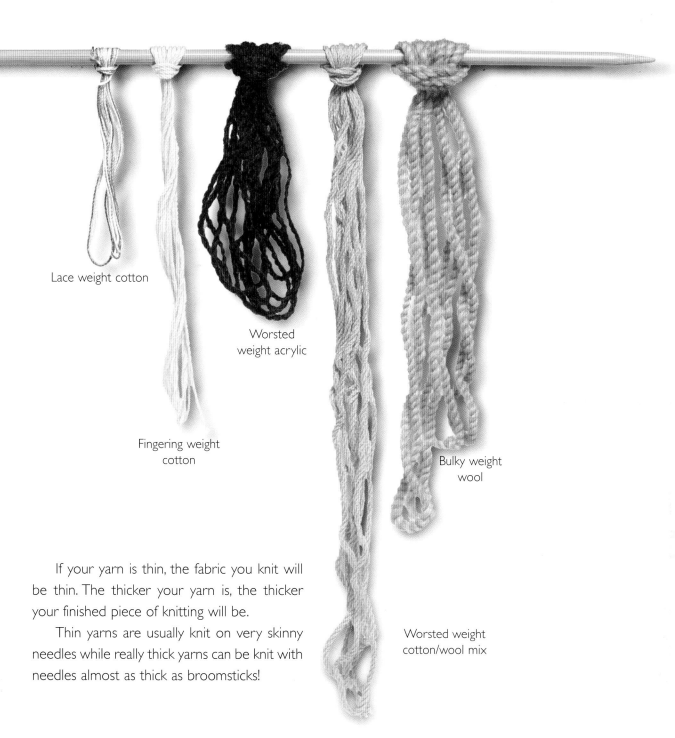

Lace weight cotton

Fingering weight cotton

Worsted weight acrylic

Bulky weight wool

Worsted weight cotton/wool mix

If your yarn is thin, the fabric you knit will be thin. The thicker your yarn is, the thicker your finished piece of knitting will be.

Thin yarns are usually knit on very skinny needles while really thick yarns can be knit with needles almost as thick as broomsticks!

Yarn Thicknesses Used in This Book

US	Australia/UK	Approximate Gauge
Sport weight, double knit, or dk	8 ply, dk, or double knit	22 sts to 4 inches (10 cm)
Worsted weight	10 ply or aran weight	20 sts to 4 inches (10 cm)
Bulky	14 ply	14 sts to 4 inches (10 cm)

Novelty Yarns

Feather eyelash

Metallic glitter

Marled yarn

Unspun

Multicolored

Knot yarn

Bouclé yarn

Knitted cord yarn

What Is Your Yarn Made From?

Yarns can be made from all sorts of different things. Some are found in nature and some are man-made. Natural fibers (or raw materials) grow on animals and in plants. They can be made into yarns by washing, preparing the fibers (pulling them apart, straightening them out, or mixing them up), and then twisting them together. Some of the animals and plants include: sheep (for wool), cotton plant (for cotton), silk worm cocoons (for silk), alpacas (for alpaca), angora goats (for mohair), angora rabbits (for angora), flax plant (for linen), and llamas (for llama).

Man-made fibers were invented by scientists. These fibers have to be made in a factory before they can be made into yarn. Some man-made yarns include acrylic and nylon.

Yarns can also be made from many other strange and wonderful things: from aluminum, plastic, and paper to Australian possum fur. They can be glittery, loopy, bumpy, smooth, fluffy, thick, thin, thick and thin all in one ball, scratchy, soft, one color or many!

When you're learning to knit, it is best to use yarn that is smooth and soft to touch. That way, your hands won't get sore and you can easily see your stitches.

Where to Buy Yarn

There are lots of places where you can buy yarn. First, look in your local phone book and see if there is a yarn shop near where you live. It's always good to be able to touch the yarn you want to buy to see if you like it. Large craft stores sometimes have a yarn section as well.

If you can't find a store close to you, you can buy your yarn over the Internet. Make sure you have your parent's permission and have them help you place your order.

If you want to make your allowance go further, keep an eye out for yarn at charity stores and garage sales. If you're lucky, you can sometimes find great yarns that someone no longer wants.

Buying Different Yarns

If you can't find, or don't want to use, the same yarns as the ones in this book, you can easily choose another yarn for your project. Look at the suggested gauge on the label of the yarn you want to use. If it's the same as the gauge for your pattern, then you can use it instead.

Caution

For the pot holder project (see page 76), you must only use 100% wool or 100% cotton in making it. Any other yarn will not keep the heat away from your hands. Acrylic and nylon may also melt into a hot liquid and stick to your skin if they accidentally catch fire.

Lessons and Projects

Casting On

The very first thing you need to do when you knit anything is to put the stitches onto your needles. This is called "casting on."

1 First, you need to make a knot with a loop in it. This is called a slipknot. Start the slipknot by making a loop of yarn.

2 Take the part of the yarn that is connected to the ball of yarn (not the end that's dangling free) and twist it behind the loop.

3 With two fingers, grab the yarn at the spot where the arrow is pointing and pull it through the loop.

4 Pull the loose end (the one that's dangling free, not the one connected to the ball of yarn) until the loop tightens up—but not too tight!

5 Put the slipknot onto one of your needles and pull the yarn that is connected to the ball so that the loop fits neatly on your needle. Now we'll add more stitches. It might feel tricky at first, but the more you practice, the easier it will be.

6 Hold the needle containing the slipknot in your left hand. The best way to hold it is with your hand over the needle. Take your empty needle in the other hand and put the tip through the slipknot and behind the left-hand needle.

7 Wind the yarn that is connected to the ball around the empty needle.

TIP

If you have trouble remembering left from right, put a temporary tattoo on the back of your left hand!

8 and 9 Using the tip of your right-hand needle, pull the yarn through the slipknot and put the new loop onto the needle in your left hand. You've made a new stitch!

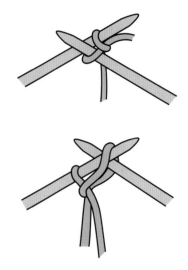

10 To cast on the rest of the stitches, put your empty needle between the last two loops on the left-hand needle instead of in the loop, as you did with the first stitch. Do not pull the new stitches too tightly. You should be able to slide them up and down your needle easily. Each loop on the left-hand needle is one stitch. Cast on 14 stitches.

The Knit Stitch

Now that you have cast on your stitches, you're ready to start knitting. There are two basic stitches in knitting: the "knit" stitch and the "purl" stitch. We will start by learning the "knit" stitch. The "purl" stitch will be discussed on page 47.

The knit stitch is a lot like casting on, except for two things: (1) You always put your needle through the loop of the stitch, never behind it. (2) You'll be adding rows of knitting instead of stitches.

Garter stitch.

1 Put the right-hand needle into the first stitch on the left-hand needle.

2 Wind the yarn around the needle exactly as you did when you casted on.

3 Using the right-hand needle, pull the loop through the first stitch.

4 Keep the new stitch on the right-hand needle. Gently move the old stitch off the end of the left-hand needle. This can feel tricky at first, but it gets easier with practice!

Congratulations, you've knit your first stitch! Knit the rest of your stitches in the same way, then switch your needles over so that the one with all the stitches is in your left hand again. Now you're ready to start the next row.

Knit 27 more rows so that you have 28 rows of knitting all together. One ridge of bumps equals two rows of knitting. When you knit every row this way, it is called "garter stitch."

Binding Off

Binding off is the most common way of finishing your knitting so that it won't come apart. Once you know how to do the knit stitch, you almost know how to bind off as well!

1 Start by knitting the first two stitches.

2 Put the tip of your left-hand needle into the first stitch that you knit on your right-hand needle. Lift the stitch up and over the top of the second stitch and off the needle. Now you should have just one stitch on your right-hand needle.

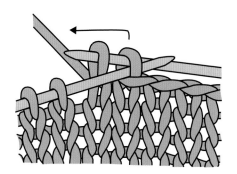

3 Knit another stitch and bind off the next stitch by lifting the first stitch over the one you knit last. Bind off all your stitches this way until you have only one stitch left on your right-hand needle.

4 To bind off the last stitch, cut your yarn at least 6 inches (about 15 cm) from your knitting. With your right-hand needle, slightly pull the last stitch until it is large enough and thread the end of your yarn through it. Remove the needle and pull the yarn firmly, but not tight enough to break it! This last step is called "fastening off."

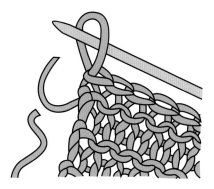

Darning In Your Ends

When you finish a piece of knitting, you'll have at least two tails of yarn hanging loose. Most of the time, the piece will also have a "right" side and a "wrong" side. The right side is the side you want people to see and the wrong side is the side you don't want people to see. To finish off your piece, you'll need to darn these loose tails into the wrong side of your knitting.

1 Thread one of the loose yarn ends through your darning needle.

2 Put the needle down through one of the threads on the wrong side of your work, then down again into the stitch next to it.

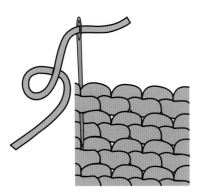

3 Keep going until you've darned through 6 or 7 stitches, pull gently, then go back the other way, darning back over the same stitches. Cut the loose thread about $1/4$ inch (about $1/2$ cm) from the knitting and you're done!

You've just finished your very first piece of knitting! Put it somewhere safe. You may want to use it in another project later on.

Now, after all that hard work, you're almost ready to knit your first project...

How to Read a Knitting Pattern

Most knitting patterns are made up of several different parts. This makes it easy for you to find the information you need.

SIZE

The measurements of your finished project.

MATERIALS

A list of the yarn, needles, and any other supplies you'll need to make your project.

GAUGE

How big your stitches need to be. We'll use your first project to learn about measuring gauge (see page 30).

ABBREVIATIONS

Most knitting patterns save space by using special short codes to mean certain things. To make sure you know what they mean, there is usually a list of these at the beginning of the pattern. We'll learn all about knitting abbreviations later on (see page 58).

PATTERN

The instructions for knitting all the pieces for your project.

FINISHING

How to put your project together.

Measuring Gauge

Measuring gauge tells you how big your stitches are and whether your stitches are the same size as the pattern's. This is especially important if you're knitting something to wear, like a sweater or a hat.

1 Put your piece of knitting down on something flat. This is very important!

2 Use your measuring tape to measure 4 inches (10 cm) across your knitting. Count how many stitches fit into those 4 inches. If you have half a stitch at the end of your 4 inches, include that half a stitch as well.

3 The number that you get is your gauge.

The gauge for the washcloth project on the next page says, "17 sts to 4 inches (10 cm) over garter stitch on size 7 needles." This means 17 stitches should fit into a 4-inch (10-cm) wide piece of knitting that you have done in garter stitch with a size 7 pair of needles.

If your piece of knitting has fewer stitches than the gauge for your pattern, try again with needles that are the next size smaller. If your piece of knitting has more stitches than the gauge for your pattern, try again with needles that are the next size larger.

TIP

If you're knitting a big project, like a sweater, always knit a square first using the same needles and yarn for that project. Use the square to measure your gauge before you start. It may seem like a lot of work, but getting the right gauge is very important if you want your knitting to turn out the same size as the pattern. Checking your gauge first can save you a lot of time later on.

PROJECT 1

Washcloth

Size

6¾ inches square (17 cm square)

Materials

- About 75 yards (68½ m) of worsted weight cotton, such as 1½ oz (43 g) Sugar'n Cream worsted weight cotton.
- A pair of size 7 knitting needles.

Gauge

17 sts to 4 inches (10 cm) over garter stitch on size 7 needles.

Pattern

1. Cast on 34 stitches.

2. Knit every stitch for 68 rows.

3. Bind off.

Finishing

Darn in the loose ends of yarn and admire your work!

Washcloths make great presents for almost any occasion, and they are a really good way to practice your knitting!

TIP

For a special gift, put your washcloth and a pretty bar of soap in a small basket and tie a ribbon on the handle in a matching color.

Overcasting

There are lots of different ways to sew your knitting together. We'll start by learning how to overcast. Overcasting is used when you want your sewing to show on the outside. You can do it with a different-colored yarn for decoration.

You'll Need:

- Two pieces of knitting you want to sew together.
- A darning needle.
- Yarn.

1 Take the two pieces of knitting and put them together with the wrong sides facing each other.

2 Thread your needle with a length of your sewing yarn about 18 to 24 inches (45 to 60 cm) long. Don't use a piece too much longer or it will get tangled up.

3 Near the edge, bring the needle through the back of your knitting to the front and pull it through, leaving a 4-inch (10-cm) tail at the back.

4 Bring the needle through your knitting from the back to the front again, about ¼ inch (½ cm) from the last spot and pull the thread through until your stitch looks neat. Do not pull too tightly.

5 Repeat step 4 around all the edges you want to sew together. If you run out of yarn, leave a 3 or 4 inch tail and keep going with a fresh piece of yarn.

6 Bring all the loose ends through to the inside of your knitting with your needle. Darn them in as you did before.

Headband

Size

This headband can be made in different sizes. For larger sizes, you just knit a longer strip. The different lengths are given in the pattern.

This comfy thick headband will keep your ears warm on cold winter days.

Materials

- About 25 yards (23 m) of bulky weight yarn, such as Patons Homespun in bulky weight: 10% mohair, 5% wool, 85% acrylic; colors 3256 (cream) and 3579 (sand). You can also use any other colorful yarn of your choice that provides the same gauge.
- A pair of size 10½ knitting needles.

Gauge

14 stitches to 4 inches (10 cm) over garter stitch on size 10½ needles.

Pattern

1. Cast on 10 stitches and knit every row until your work measures:
   - To fit someone aged 7–10 years old: 16 inches (41 cm).
   - Ages 11–14: 17 inches (43 cm).
   - Ages 16–adult size small: 18 inches (46 cm).
   - Adult size medium: 19 inches (48 cm).
   - Adult size large: 20 inches (51 cm).
2. Bind off.

Finishing

Overcast the short ends together and darn in the loose ends. Put it on and go play in the snow!

How to Make Tassels and Fringes

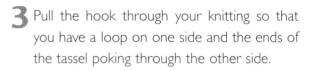

Tassels make a great decoration on lots of different projects, from the tops of hats to the corners of cushions, and anything else in between!

You'll Need:

- A crochet hook.
- Some yarn.
- A piece of knitting you want to attach your tassels to.

1 Cut three or four pieces of yarn a bit more than twice as long as you want your finished tassels to be. Fold the pieces in half.

2 Hold your knitting sideways so you can see what you're doing on both sides of the knitting. Put your crochet hook through the knitting where you want your tassel to be. Put the yarn for your tassel over the hook.

3 Pull the hook through your knitting so that you have a loop on one side and the ends of the tassel poking through the other side.

4 Thread the loose ends through the loop and pull firmly to tighten the tassel.

5 Make a row of tassels for a fringe!

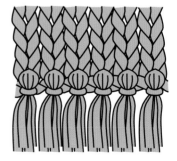

TIP

If you're making tassels at the end of your knitting, put the crochet hook at least one row up from the edge. That way the edge will stay straight and neat.

How to Sew on a Snap Fastener

You'll Need:

- A sewing needle that will fit through the holes on your snap.
- Sewing thread.

1 Cut a piece of thread about 36 inches (91 cm) long. Thread your needle and pull the thread so that it is doubled.

2 Sew three or four small stitches on top of each other at the spot where you want to put the snap. This will fasten the end of your thread. Try to catch just the top of your knitting so that the stitches won't show on the other side.

3 Take apart your snap. You'll see that it has two pieces: one with a bump and one with a dip. Both pieces have four little holes around the edge. You will sew the snap to your knitting through these holes.

4 Thread your needle through one of the little holes on the snap. Make sure that the side that snaps together with the other piece faces up. Push it all the way down the thread until it is sitting where you want it to be on your knitting.

5 Bring the needle down into your knitting next to the snap outside the hole. Then bring the needle up through the hole and pull it through. Do this about 6 times. Then bring your needle down into the knitting and have it come up at the next hole.

6 Sew the snap to your knitting at each hole. After the last hole, sew 3 or 4 stitches on top of each other. Cut your thread. Sew on the second piece of your snap in the same way. Make sure that the second piece lines up with the first piece.

Sunglasses Case

Size

4 × 8 inches (10 × 20 cm)

Materials

- About 100 yards (91 m) of double knit yarn in one color for the main part of the case, such as 1¾ oz (50 g) Jo Sharp 8 ply weight wool in purple and a scrap of a second color yarn for sewing it together.
- 1 × ¼ inch (2½ × 1 cm) snap fastener.
- A pair of size 6 knitting needles.

Gauge

22 stitches to 4 inches (10 cm) over garter stitch on size 6 needles.

Pattern

1. Cast on 22 stitches and knit every stitch for 88 rows.
2. Bind off.
3. Repeat steps 1 and 2 to make a second rectangle.

Finishing

1. Darn in the loose ends.
2. Overcast the two pieces together on three sides, making sure to leave one short end open so you can put your glasses in.
3. Make tassels on the two bottom corners.
4. Sew the snap fastener to the center at the top so the case can be kept closed.

Keep your sunglasses safe from scratches in a knitted case! This case is made from two rectangles of knitting sewn together with tassels added at the corners. If you don't like the tassels, they can be left off.

Joining a New Ball of Yarn

When you run out of yarn or want to start a new color, you'll need to join a new ball of yarn to your knitting.

1 Knit to the end of your row. It's always best to join a new ball of yarn at the end of a row.

2 Tie your new yarn together with the old yarn. Tie it loosely because you'll need to undo it later on.

3 Keep knitting!

4 When you've finished your knitting, untie the knot and darn the ends into the back of your knitting as you did with the loose ends on the projects you've already made.

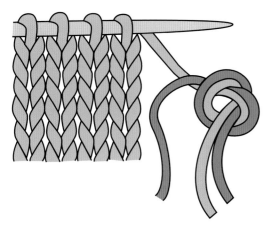

Backstitch

Another way of sewing pieces of knitting together is to use backstitch. This way will not show your stitches on the outside of your work.

You'll Need:

- The pieces of knitting you want to sew together.
- A darning needle.
- The same yarn that you used to knit your project.

1 Cut a piece of yarn about 18 to 24 inches (46 to 60 cm) long and thread it onto your darning needle.

2 Take your pieces of knitting and place them with the right sides together so that your project is "inside out."

3 Bring the needle up through both pieces of knitting near the edge and about ¼ inch (½ cm) from the place you want to start sewing.

4 Then bring the darning needle down through both pieces of knitting at Point #1 in the picture, then back up at Point #2. Then bring the needle back down through the place where you first brought the needle up in step 3. Try to keep your stitches no bigger than ¼ inch (½ cm), unless you're using very thick yarn. Do not pull too tightly.

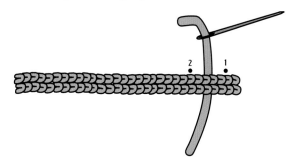

5 Keep sewing like this, bringing the needle down through the knitting at Point #1 and up through the knitting at Point #2.

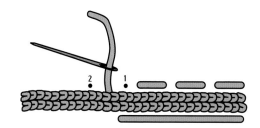

6 When you've finished sewing your seam, darn the loose ends in using your darning needle.

Doll Blanket

Size

7½ × 11 inches (20 × 28 cm)

Materials

● 1 oz (28 g) each in three different colors, such as Baby Soft sportweight yarn in colors 106 (pastel blue), 157 (pastel yellow), and 293 (twinkle).*

● A pair of size 5 knitting needles.

* Name one color "A," one color "B," and the last one "C." It doesn't matter which one you choose as A, B, or C. When the pattern says to use color A, use the yarn that you named color A and so on with the other two colors.

Gauge

22½ sts to 4 inches (10 cm) over garter stitch on size 6 needles.

Pattern

1. Cast on 44 sts and work in garter stitch (knit every stitch) in stripes as follows:

   20 rows of color A

   20 rows of color B

   20 rows of color C

   20 rows of color A

   20 rows of color B

   20 rows of color C

2. Bind off.

Finishing

Darn in all the loose ends.

Knitting stripes is a great way to practice joining a new ball of yarn.

Doll

This doll used lavender for the pants and hair bow, light green for the shirt, pale pink for the skin, dark brown for the hair, and black for the eyes and mouth.

Size

Approximately 9 inches (23 cm) tall when stuffed. Stuffing usually stretches the knitting slightly.

Materials

- About 50 yards (46 m) each of double knit yarn in various colors. (Choose a yarn that suggests a gauge of 22 sts to 4 inches/10 cm on the label.)
- A pair of size 3 knitting needles.
- Polyester stuffing (available at your local craft shop).
- Optional: Wobbly eyes, fabric glue, and fabric paint for the face.

Gauge

26 sts to 4 inches (10 cm) over garter stitch on size 3 needles.

Pattern

FRONT

1. Using your pants color yarn, cast on 18 stitches and knit 44 rows in garter stitch (every row knit).

2. Change to your shirt color yarn and knit 24 rows.

3. Change to your skin color yarn and knit 16 rows.

4. Change to your hair color yarn and knit 16 rows.

5. Bind off.

BACK

6. Using your pants color yarn, cast on 18 stitches and knit 44 rows in garter stitch.

7. Change to your shirt color yarn and knit 24 rows.

This little doll can be made in any color you like. Try making one in your favorite team colors! For a boy doll, just leave the pigtails off. It might look hard compared to the projects you've knit so far, but don't worry, it's made from simple rectangles. Decide which color you want to use for the different parts of your doll.

8. Change to hair color yarn and knit 30 rows.

9. Bind off.

ARMS

10. Using skin color yarn, cast on 14 sts and knit 8 rows in garter stitch.

11. Change to your shirt color yarn and knit 26 rows.

12. Bind off.

13. Repeat steps 10 to 12 to make another arm.

Finishing

1. Using the same color yarn as your knitting, bring the right sides (the sides you want to show on the outside when the doll is finished) of the front piece and back piece together and backstitch the sides together. Use a fairly small stitch close to the edges. You can use the loose threads on the smaller pieces to sew them together, if they're long enough. Turn the body inside out.

2. Gather the top of the head by sewing big stitches close to the edge. Pull it tight and tie the yarn together. If there's still a hole in the top, use the end of your gathering yarn to overcast it closed and then poke the ends through to the inside.

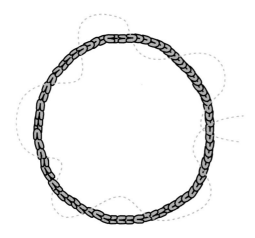

3. Stuff the doll's body and overcast the bottom seam.

4. Wind a piece of pale pink yarn several times around the body where you changed from shirt color to skin color. Pull slightly to make the doll's neck. Tie a knot and darn in the ends.

When you darn in the ends on something you've stuffed, you can make 2 or 3 stitches on top of each other. Cut the thread 2 inches (5 cm) from your knitting and poke the end inside.

5. Using a backstitch, sew a line between the legs. Pull your stitches tight so that the legs come out round. Stop a few rows before you reach the doll's shirt.

6. Fold the arm pieces in half with the right sides together and sew the long sides together using backstitch. Sew the cast-on edge seam as well. Turn the arms inside out.

7. Stuff the arms and overcast them to the body about ½ inch (1½ cm) below the neck.

8. Make tassels for pigtails on both sides of the head. If you want your doll to have a ponytail, you can make one tassel at the back of the head instead. Or, you can have no tassels for a boy doll.

9. Cut small pieces of yarn and use them to tie bows on the pigtails.

10. You can make the face using puffy fabric paint, stick-on felt, or use fabric glue to stick on tiny googly eyes. If you know how to embroider, you can also sew the face on (see page 45).

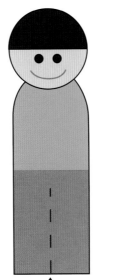

Backstitch here to make the legs

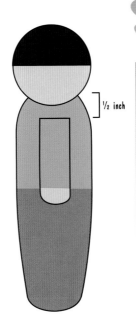

½ inch

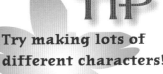

Try making lots of different characters! You can knit a robot from shiny silver yarn—don't gather the neck or the top of the head; just cast off and sew it closed. You can also make a baby from pink yarn or a clown with different colors on every piece. Or you can make your doll brown and knit small rectangles for dog's ears! Let your imagination run wild!

The Purl Stitch

The "purl" stitch is the other stitch used in knitting. If you purl every row, it will look just like garter stitch (knit every row). But you can use the knit stitch and purl stitch together to make hundreds of different effects! A basic knit and purl stitch combination is called a "stockinette stitch." Later on, we will learn a different kind of knit and purl stitch called a "rib stitch" (see page 52).

1 Put your right-hand needle into the first stitch. Insert it from the back of the stitch to the front.

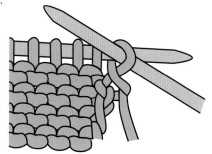

2 Wind the yarn around the needle. Make sure the yarn goes around the needle the way it is shown in the picture.

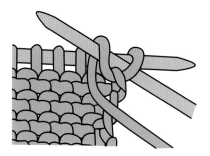

3 Using the right-hand needle, pull the yarn through the loop.

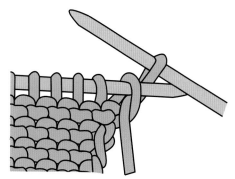

4 Carefully drop the old stitch off the left-hand needle.

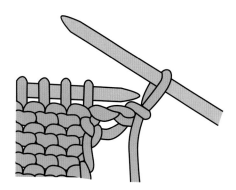

Congratulations, you've knit your first purl stitch! To make more, repeat steps 1 to 4.

Stockinette Stitch

Stockinette stitch is the most basic combination of knit and purl stitches. It is worked following the instructions below.

1 1st row: Knit every stitch.

2 2nd row: Purl every stitch.

3 Repeat these two rows.

To count how many rows of stockinette stitch you have, look at the front of your knitting. One row of V's is one row of knitting.

Scrunchie

Materials

- Scraps of double knit weight yarn, such as Cleckheaton Country 8 ply weight and Jo Sharp Country 8 ply weight wools in various colors.
- A pair of size 6 knitting needles.
- 9 inches (23 cm) of ¼-inch (½-cm) wide elastic.

Knit a hair scrunchie to match your favorite outfit—or make one for your mom!

Gauge

22 sts to 4 inches (10 cm) over stockinette stitch on size 6 needles.

Pattern

1. Cast on 10 sts.

2. 1st row: Knit every stitch.

3. 2nd row: Purl every stitch.

4. Keep working in stockinette stitch until your knitting is 11 inches (28 cm) long.

Finishing

1. With the right sides (the sides you want to show on the outside) facing each other, backstitch the short ends together. Turn it right-side out.

2. With the wrong sides facing each other (the sides you don't want to show), fold your knitting so that the long sides are together. You'll have a piece of knitting that looks a bit like a donut.

3. Overcast the long edges together but leave a small hole.

4. Thread your piece of elastic through the scrunchie and sew the ends together. Overcast the small hole to close it.

TIP

To make it easier to thread the elastic through the scrunchie, attach a large safety pin to the end of the elastic and push the pin through the scrunchie.

Ribbing

Ribbing is another way of combining knit and purl stitches. Here, we'll put knit and purl stitches next to each other in the same row. The rib stitch we're going to learn first is called "Knit One, Purl One" rib.

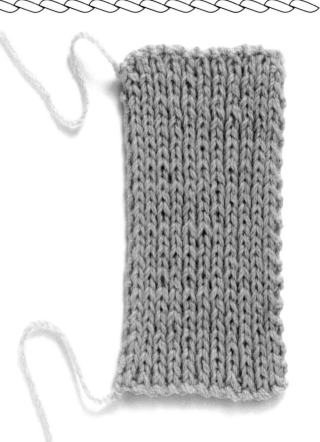

1 Cast on 15 stitches.

1ST ROW

2 Knit one stitch.

3 Bring your yarn to the front of your knitting under the right-hand needle. Make sure that your yarn is between the stitch you just knit and the next one that you will knit on your left-hand needle.

4 Purl one stitch.

5 Take your yarn to the back of your knitting between the stitches.

6 Knit one stitch.

7 Repeat steps 2 to 5 until you reach the end of the row.

2ND ROW

8 Knit 2 stitches.

9 Bring your yarn to the front of your knitting between the stitches.

10 Purl one stitch.

11 Take your yarn to the back of your knitting between the stitches

12 Knit one stitch.

13 Repeat steps 2 to 5 until you have one stitch left, then knit the last stitch.

14 Repeat rows 1 and 2 until your knitting is long enough.

Twisted Cord

You can used twisted cords for all sorts of things, from shoelaces to hair ribbons and even to tease your cat!

1 Cut a piece of yarn 2½ times longer than the length of your finished cord. For example, if your pattern says to make a twisted cord 10 inches (25 cm) long, you'll need to cut a piece of yarn 25 inches (64 cm) long.

2 Fold your yarn in half and tie the ends together tightly.

3 Hook one end over a door knob, close it in a drawer, or put it anywhere that will hold it tightly while you're twisting it.

4 Slip a knitting needle (or a pencil or a crochet hook) through the other end of your loop and walk away until your yarn is tight. Start twisting your yarn by spinning the knitting needle. Keep going until the yarn tries to twist back on itself. When it starts doing this, very carefully fold the twisted yarn in half and let it twist up on itself.

5 Take the end of your yarn from the doorknob and tie a knot at the end. It won't come undone because the knot holds it together and stops it from untwisting.

6 Measure your twisted cord and tie a knot where your pattern says to. For example, if you're making a 10-nch (25-cm) long cord, tie a knot 10 inches (25 cm) from the first knot. Trim the ends neatly about 1 inch (2½ cm) from each knot so that they won't come undone.

TIP

Try making a cord from more than one color for a candy stripe effect!

Amulet Bag

Size

2 × 3 inches (5 × 7½ cm), not including the strap

Materials

- Scraps of double knit weight yarn, such as Jo Sharp 8 ply weight wool.
- A pair of size 6 knitting needles.
- One ¼-inch (½-cm) snap fastener.
- Optional: One ½-inch (1½-cm) button.

Gauge

22 sts to 4 inches (10 cm) over stockinette stitch on size 6 needles.

PATTERN

1. Cast on 13 sts.

2. 1st row: Knit 1 stitch, purl 1 stitch, knit 1 stitch. Keep working purl 1, knit 1 until you get to the end of the row.

3. 2nd row: Knit 2 stitches, purl 1 stitch, knit 1 stitch. Keep working purl 1, knit 1 until you have one stitch left, then knit the last stitch.

4. Repeat rows 1 and 2 once more. (This stitch is called Knit 1, Purl 1 rib.)

5. Change to stockinette stitch (knit 1 row, purl 1 row) and work until your work measures 5 inches (13 cm) from the very beginning.

6. Work 14 rows in Knit 1, Purl 1 rib to make the bag's flap.

7. Bind off.

Finishing

1. Fold the cast-on edge of the knitting up until it is level with the beginning of the flap (see illustration on the right).

This little bag can be worn as a necklace to keep your small treasures safe. You can put anything in it, from your favorite precious stone to a key to lip gloss!

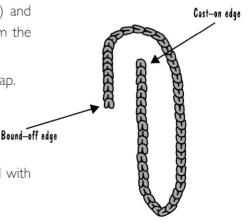

Cast-on edge

Bound-off edge

2. Make about 35½ inches (90 cm) of twisted cord. Tie a knot at both ends and trim the yarn 2 inches (5 cm) from the knot so that it looks like you have a tassel on each end.

3. Line up one end of the twisted cord, just above the knot, along one side of the bag. Overcast the cord and the sides of the bag together. Stop right where the bag flap begins. Repeat on the other side.

TIP

Sew a ½-inch (1½-cm) button in the middle of the outside flap. Sew the snap fastener in the same area just under the flap so that the flap can stay closed.

How to Make Pom-poms

Pom-poms are great for decorating your knitting. All you need are scraps of yarn to make them. You can buy a pom-pom maker from your craft or yarn store, or you can make one following the instructions below.

You'll Need:

- Two circles of light cardboard, such as old cereal boxes. Your circles will need to be the same size as your finished pom-poms. For example, if your pattern says to make 2-inch (5-cm) pom-poms, you'll need circles of cardboard that measure 2 inches (5 cm) across.
- A pair of scissors.
- A darning needle.
- Some yarn.

1 Cut a hole in the middle of your cardboard circles. The holes should be half the width of the circle.

2 Put the cardboard disks next to each other and wind yarn around them until you've filled up the hole in the middle. Use your darning needle to help get the yarn through the hole when it gets too small.

3 Using a pair of scissors, cut the yarn all the way around the edge. Make sure you've cut all the threads.

4 Cut a piece of yarn several feet long. Put it between the two cardboard disks and tie it very tightly around the middle of your pom-pom. You'll probably need an adult to help you tie it tight enough. Carefully pull the cardboard disks off your pom-pom. If it's too hard to pull the disks off, then you can cut them. Trim your pom-pom to make it nice and neat.

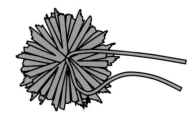

5 To attach your pom-pom to your knitting, use a piece of yarn that is 3 or 4 feet (about 90 to 120 cm) long. Find the middle of your piece of yarn and tie it around the pom-pom. Use the ends of the yarns to sew it to your knitting.

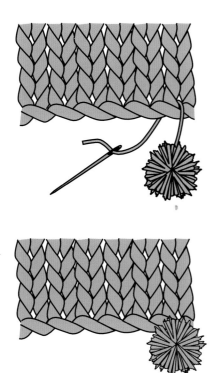

TIP

If you are sewing a pom-pom to your knitting, wind the sewing yarn once around the whole pom-pom before you darn in the ends. That way, the pom-pom won't pull loose. The fluffiness of the pom-pom will hide the sewing yarn.

Ribbed Scarf

This scarf is knit in a stitch called "knit 3, purl 3 ribbing." This makes a nice, warm, squishy fabric that will keep your neck cozy in the coldest weather.

Size

Approximately 3 × 63 inches (8 × 160 cm) long, not including the pom-poms.

Materials

- For the scarf: About 330 yards (302 m) of double knit weight yarn, such as 5¼ oz (150 g) Cleckheaton Country 8 ply weight Tweeds in color 1806 (tan tweed). For the pom-poms: 75 yards (69 m) of double knit weight yarn, such as 1¾ oz (50 g) Cleckheaton Country 8 ply weight in color 0006 (black).
- A pair of size 6 knitting needles.

Gauge

Gauge doesn't matter. It is fine if your scarf is a little wider than the pattern, but you might need to buy extra yarn to make it the same length as the one in the pattern. The suggested gauge for the yarn is 22 stitches to 4 inches (10 cm) over stockinette stitch on size 6 needles. The finished scarf is only 3 inches (8 cm) wide because the ribbing pulls it inward.

Abbreviations

K = Knit

P = Purl

When the instructions say K3, this means you knit 3 stitches.

When the instructions say P3, this means you purl 3 stitches.

Continued on page 60.

Abbreviations

Abbreviations in knitting are special ways to shorten instructions. Without them, some patterns can be very long and complicated. Abbreviations help make reading them easier and save paper. Check the list on the left to see what the abbreviations for this pattern mean.

Continued from page 58.

Pattern

1. Cast on 33 sts.

2. 1st row: K3, *P3, K3. Repeat from * to end of row.

3. 2nd row: P3, *K3, P3. Repeat from * to end of row.

Note

When a pattern says "Repeat from *," find the first * in the row and repeat the instructions that are after it.

4. Repeat rows 1 and 2 until your scarf measures 63 inches (160 cm), or however long you want it to be.

Finishing

1. Darn in all loose ends following the ribbed stripes on the wrong side.

2. If you want to, make six 2-inch (5-cm) diameter pom-poms. Sew three to each end of your scarf.

Simple Decrease

Sometimes you'll need to make fewer stitches in your knitting. This is called "decreasing." It is used to make different shapes.

1 "Knit 2 together" is one kind of decrease that can be used in lots of different projects. To "knit 2 together" means exactly that: you'll be knitting two stitches together as if they were only one stitch.

2 Put your right-hand needle into the second stitch on the left-hand needle and then through the first stitch. Knit them as you would if you were working the "knit" stitch. You now have one less stitch!

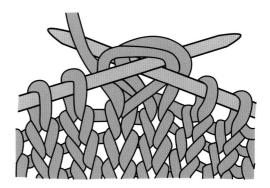

Cat Toy

Size

2 × 3½ inches (5 × 9 cm) wide.

Gauge

The gauge doesn't matter for this little cat toy. If it's bigger or smaller than the pattern says, it won't make much difference to your cat!

Materials

- Scraps of worsted weight or double knit yarn in red and lavender.
- A pair of size 6 knitting needles.
- One jingle bell about ½ inch (1½ cm) in diameter.

Abbreviations

K = Knit

K2tog = Knit 2 stitches together

Sts = Stitches

Pattern

1. Using red, cast on 22 sts.

2. 1st row: Knit.

3. 2nd row: K2tog, K to the last 2 sts, K2tog.

4. Repeat rows 1 and 2 until you have 4 sts left.

5. K 1 row.

6. K2tog twice.

7. K2tog.

8. Cut your yarn leaving a tail about 4 inches long. Thread the tail through the last stitch and close the stitch by tugging gently on the end of the yarn. This is called "fastening off."

Most cats can't resist this toy! It makes a great treat for your pets, or a gift for your favorite cat owner.

Finishing

1. Darn in all the loose ends.

2. Make a 4-inch (10-cm) long fringe along the cast-on edge.

3. Tie the center of a long strand of yarn on the top point of the toy. You may need a crochet hook to bring the yarn through. Thread on the bell and tie the ends of the yarn together. Tease your cat.

Knitted Appliqué (Say it like this: Ah-PLEH-kay)

You can make all kinds of pictures and designs by sewing knitted shapes onto a background. The only limit is your imagination! The best way to sew your pieces is to use a "running stitch."

You'll Need:

- Background fabric, such as a bigger piece of knitting, felt, or thick woven fabric.
- Pins.
- A darning needle.
- Sewing yarn in your choice of color.

1 Pin your shapes to the background fabric. If you have lots of pieces to sew on, choose one piece to start with. Each shape is called an "appliqué piece."

2 Thread your darning needle with a length of yarn about 18 inches long. (If your yarn is too long, it will tangle.)

3 Place your needle behind the fabric and the appliqué piece. It should line up near the edge of the appliqué piece. Push the needle up through both pieces.

5 About ¼ inch (½ cm) further along, push the needle back down through the appliqué piece and the background piece. Pull the yarn through until you have a neat stitch on the front.

6 Keep sewing up and down until you get back to where you started sewing. Take out the pins as you sew.

7 Darn in the ends of the sewing yarn and admire your work!

4 Pull your needle and thread through and leave a 4-inch (10-cm) tail on the back. You can darn it in later.

TIP

You can use knitted appliqué to decorate plain sweaters and hats that you buy at the store. Draw a picture of your design, knit the shapes, and sew them on!

House Cushion

Size

12 inches (30 cm) square

Materials

- 330 yards (302 m) of red double knit weight yarn for the background, such as 5 oz (142 g) Patons Totem 8 ply weight in color 1221 (cherry).
- Scraps of white, blue, and yellow double knit weight yarn for the house, such as Cleckheaton Country 8 ply weight in colors 0288 (royal), 0003 (white), and 1085 (gold).
- One 12-inch (30-cm) square pillow form. A pillow form looks like a regular pillow without a cover.
- A pair of size 6 knitting needles.

Gauge

22 sts to 4 inches (10 cm) over stockinette stitch on size 6 needles.

Abbreviations

K = Knit

K2tog = Knit 2 stitches together

Sts = Stitches

St st = Stockinette stitch

Pattern
CUSHION

1. Using the red yarn, cast on 66 sts and knit in stockinette stitch for 12 inches (30 cm).

2. Bind off.

3. Repeat steps 1 and 2 to make another one.

Continued on page 66.

Continued from page 65.

HOUSE

4. Using the yellow yarn, cast on 26 sts and work 30 rows st st.

5. Bind off.

ROOF

6. Using the blue yarn, cast on 32 sts.

7. 1st row: K2tog, K to last 2 sts, K2tog.

8. 2nd row: Knit.

9. Repeat steps 6 and 7 until you reach K2tog twice.

10. Next row: K2tog, then fasten off.

WINDOWS

11. Using the white yarn, cast on 6 sts and knit 10 rows.

12. Bind off.

13. Repeat steps 11 and 12 to make another window.

DOOR

14. Using the white yarn, cast on 6 sts and knit 20 rows.

15. Bind off.

POM-POMS

16. Using the red, yellow, and blue yarns together, make four 2-inch pom-poms.

Finishing

1. Following the photograph, sew the windows and doors to the main part of the house, then sew the house to one of the red pieces. Make sure that the house is slightly below the middle of the red piece. Place the roof over the house so that it covers a little bit of the top. Sew the roof on.

2. With the right sides (the sides you want to show when you're finished) facing, sew the red pieces together around three sides using backstitch.

3. Turn your piece inside out and put the pillow form inside the cover.

4. Overcast the last side. Sew a pom-pom to each corner.

TIP

You can make your cushion in any color. Use your favorite colors or choose colors to match the room you want to use it in.

Teddy Bear Puppet

Size

About 4 × 8½ inches (10 × 22 cm)

Materials

- 110 yards (101 m) of double knit weight yarn in dark brown, such as 1¾ oz (50 g) Jo Sharp worsted weight yarn in color 506 (chestnut).
- A pair of size 6 knitting needles.
- Small amount of toy filling for ears.
- Scraps of craft felt in black, light brown, and white for the face.
- Fabric glue.
- An old plastic shopping bag or a piece of sandwich wrap.

Gauge

22 sts to 4 inches (10 cm) over stockinette stitch.

Abbreviations

K2tog = Knit 2 stitches together

Sts = Stitches

St st = Stockinette stitch

Pattern

BODY

1. Cast on 24 sts and knit 12 rows in garter st (knit every row).

2. Continue in stockinette stitch until you've knit 7 inches (18 cm) from the cast-on edge. Now you're ready to shape the top.

3. 1st row: K2tog, knit to the last 2 stitches, k2tog.

4. 2nd row: Purl.

5. Repeat steps 3 and 4 until you have 12 stitches left, ending on a purl row.

Continued on page 70.

Continued from page 68.

6. Bind off.

7. Repeat steps 1 to 6 to make the other side of the body.

EARS

8. Cast on 10 sts and work 8 rows st st. Now you're ready to decrease the top.

9. 1st row: K2tog, knit to the last 2 stitches, k2tog.

10. 2nd row: Purl.

11. Repeat steps 9 and 10 once more. You should now have 6 stitches left.

12. Bind off.

13. Repeat steps 8 to 12 until you have three more ear pieces.

Finishing

1. With the right sides facing each other, sew the 2 body pieces together around the edges. Do not sew the bottom. Turn it right-side out.

2. Sew two of the ear pieces together as follows: place the right sides facing each other, join the top and sides together, and turn it inside out. Stuff them lightly with filling. Do the same with the other two pieces. Sew the ears to the shaped sides of the bear's head.

3. Put a piece of plastic from an old shopping bag or sandwich wrap inside your puppet. Cut the face of your teddy bear from the felt and stick it on with fabric glue.

4. Try making puppets of your own design! Knit small triangles for cat's ears, long rectangles for dog's ears, or make a person by leaving the ears off and adding pigtails made from tassels!

If you have trouble getting your face pieces to stick, put a piece of plastic over them. Then put a heavy book on top and leave it there for a couple of days, or until the glue has completely dried.

Simple Increase: The Half Hitch

Sometimes you need to add stitches to your knitting. This is called "increasing." There are lots of different ways to increase in knitting. The easiest way is called the "half hitch" increase.

1 Work to the part of your pattern where it says to increase one stitch. Twist a loop in your yarn and put it on your right-hand needle.

2 That's it! On the next row, treat the loop as if it were a regular stitch and knit it following the instructions for your pattern.

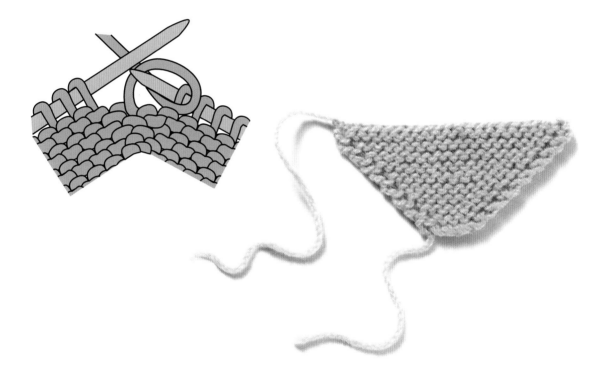

Kerchief

Size

13 inches (33 cm) wide: To fit ages 6–15.

Materials

- About 100 yards (91 m) of double knit weight yarn for your main color and scraps of two other colors for the stripes, such as Cleckheaton Country 8 ply weight for the light-pink kerchief and Jo Sharp 8 ply for the darker one.
- A pair of size 6 knitting needles.

Gauge

22 sts to 4 inches (10 cm) worked in garter stitch on size 6 needles.

Abbreviations

K = Knit

Sts = Stitches

Pattern

1. Using your main color, cast on 3 sts.

2. 1st row: K1, increase, k1, increase, k1.

3. 2nd row: Knit to the end.

4. 3rd row: K1, increase, knit until there is one st left, increase, k1.

5. 4th row: Knit to the end.

6. Repeat steps 4 and 5 until you have 59 stitches.

7. Continue increasing as before and work stripes as follows: 2 rows for the thin stripe, 10 rows for the thick stripe, 2 rows for the second thin stripe.

8. Bind off.

Finishing

1. Darn in the loose ends.

2. Cut two pieces of yarn 37½ inches (95 cm) long. Tie the center of one piece of yarn to one corner of the cast-off row. Tie the loose ends together. Make another tie the same way at the other corner of the cast off row.

Kite Bookmark

Materials

- Scraps of worsted weight or double knit weight yarn.
- A pair of size 6 or 7 knitting needles.

Gauge

Doesn't matter!

Abbreviations

K = Knit

Inc = Increase one stitch

K2tog = Knit 2 stitches together

Sts = Stitches

Pattern

1. Cast on 2 sts.

2. K1, inc, k1.

3. Next row: Knit.

4. Next row: K1, inc, k to the last st, inc, k1.

5. Repeat steps 3 and 4 until you have 19 sts.

6. K 1 row.

7. K2tog, k to last 2 sts, k2tog.

8. Next row: Knit to the end.

9. Repeat steps 7 and 8 until you have 3 sts left.

10. K 1 row.

11. Next row: K1, k2tog.

12. Next row: K2tog.

13. Cut the yarn, leaving it 12 inches (30 cm) long.

14. Fasten off, leaving the yarn long for the kite tail.

Finishing

1. Darn in the cast on end.

2. Tie little bits of colored yarn to cast off end for the kite tail.

Yarn Over

Yarn overs are a way of making holes in your knitting without your work coming apart. Yarn overs can be used to make extra stitches, buttonholes, give your knitting a lacy look, or makes holes so that you can thread a drawstring through.

1 To make a yarn over, bring your yarn to the front of your knitting as shown in the picture, then knit your next stitch. This makes an extra loop over your needle. The extra loop is the yarn over. On the next row, knit the yarn over as if it were a regular stitch.

2 If you count your stitches, you'll see that you now have one more than you did before. If you want to keep the same number of stitches, work your yarn over, then, instead of knitting the next stitch, knit the next two stitches together.

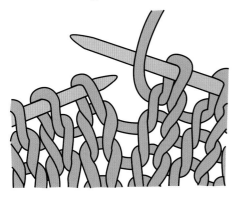

Pot Holder

This double-thick pot holder makes a great gift for people who like to cook.

Caution:

Use only 100% wool or 100% cotton in making it! Any other yarn will not keep the heat away from your hands. Some yarn, such as acrylic and nylon, may also melt into a hot liquid and stick to your skin if they accidentally catch fire.

Size

9 inch (23 cm) square

Materials

- 110 yards (101 m) each of double knit weight wool in two colors, such as 1¾ oz (50 g) Jo Sharp 8 ply weight yarn in colors 322 (ginger) and 703 (ivory).
- A pair of size 6 knitting needles.

Gauge

22 sts to 4 inches (10 cm) over garter stitch on size 6 needles.

Abbreviations

K = Knit

K2tog = Knit 2 stitches together

Yo = Yarn over

Sts = Stitches

Pattern

1. Cast on 2 sts.

2. For every row, k1, yo, k to the end. At the end of every row, you'll have one more stitch than the row before. Continue increasing until you have 68 sts, then begin decreasing.

3. Next row: K1, yo, k2tog, k to the last 3 sts, k2tog, k1.

4. Repeat step 3 until you have 4 sts left.

5. Next row: K2tog twice.

6. Last row: K2tog.

7. Fasten off.

8. Repeat steps 1 to 7 to make another piece.

Finishing

1. Using a strand of each yarn together, sew the two pieces together through the holes made by the yarn overs.

2. Cut the yarn when you get to each corner, leaving 4 inches (10 cm) extra at each end.

3. Tie knots at corners and cut the yarn, leaving ½ inch (about 1½ cm) ends. Don't leave them longer or they might be dangerous when you lift pots off the stove top.

Drawstring Purse

Size

Approximately 5 × 7½ inches (13 × 19 cm)

Materials

- About 110 yards (101 m) of double knit weight yarn, such as Cleckheaton Country 8 ply weight in colors 1085 (gold), 2180 (emerald), and 1979 (regal).
- A pair of size 6 knitting needles.
- Optional: Two pony beads, or other beads with large holes.

Gauge

22 sts to 4 inches (10 cm) over st st on size 6 needles.

Abbreviations

K = Knit

K2tog = Knit 2 stitches together

Yo = Yarn over

Sts = Stitches

St st = Stockinette stitch

Pattern

1. Cast on 60 sts.

2. Work in st st for 7 inches (17¾ cm).

3. K 4 rows.

4. Next row: K1, * yo, k2tog. Repeat from * to the last st, k1.

5. K 3 rows.

6. Bind off.

Finishing

1. Fold the bag in half with the row of holes at the top and the right sides together. Sew the sides and the bottom using backstitch. Turn the bag right-side out.

2. Make a twisted cord about 12 inches (30 cm) long and thread it through the holes to make the drawstring. You can thread on two pony beads before tying the ends of the drawstring together.

Fashion Doll Dress

Size

To fit any 11½ inch (29 cm) tall fashion doll

Materials

- Scraps of double weight yarn in two colors, such as Cleckheaton Country 8 ply weight in colors 0003 (white), 1858 (dusty pink), and 1085 (gold).
- A pair of size 6 knitting needles.

Gauge

22 sts to 4 inches (10 cm) over st st on size 6 needles.

This little dress is knit from the bottom of the skirt up. It's made in one piece with a seam up the back.

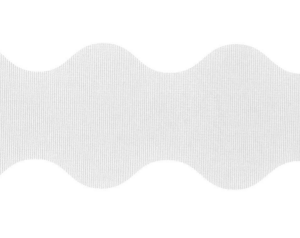

Abbreviations

K = Knit

K2tog = Knit 2 stitches together

Yo = Yarn over

Sts = Stitches

St st = Stockinette stitch

Pattern

1. Using skirt color, cast on 33 sts and knit 10 rows in garter stitch.

2. Continue in st st until work measures 4 inches (10 cm) from the cast-on edge.

3. Knit 2 rows in garter stitch.

4. Next row: K1, * yo, k2tog. Repeat from * to the end of the row.

5. K 1 row, then change to shirt color and knit 1½ inches (4 cm) in garter stitch.

6. Next row: K1, * yo, k2tog. Repeat from * to the end of the row.

7. Bind off.

Finishing

1. Darn in all loose ends.

2. Fold the dress in half with the right sides facing each other and sew the seam down the back using backstitch. Turn it right-side out.

3. Thread yarn through the eyelet holes around the top and the waist. Put it on your doll and tie in a bow at the back in both places.

Backpack

Size

Approximately 10 inches (25 cm) square

Materials

- Approximately 330 yards (302 m) of double knit weight cotton, such as Cleckheaton's Click Clack Cotton 8 ply weight in color 1209 (puce pink), and scraps of a different color yarn.
- A pair of size 6 knitting needles.

Gauge

22 sts to 4 inches (10 cm) over st st on size 6 needles.

Abbreviations

K = Knit

K2tog = Knit 2 stitches together

Sts = Stitches

St st = Stockinette stitch

Yo = Yarn over

Pattern

BAG

1. Cast on 55 sts and work in st st for 9 inches.

2. K 6 rows in garter st.

3. Next row: K1 * yo, k2tog. Repeat from * to the end of the row.

4. K 5 rows.

5. Bind off.

6. Repeat steps 1 to 5 to make another piece.

FLAP

7. Cast on 22 sts and knit every row in garter st for 6 inches (15 cm).

8. Bind off.

STRAPS

9. Cast on 8 sts and knit every row in garter st until your work measures 20 inches (51 cm).

10. Bind off.

11. Repeat steps 9 and 10 to make another one.

Finishing

1. Darn in all your loose ends.

2. Place the bag pieces together with the right sides facing each other and the row of holes at the top. Sew together the sides and across the bottom using backstitch.

3. Overcast the cast-on edge of the flap to the back of the bag just below the row of holes.

4. Overcast the straps to the bag as shown in the illustration on the right.

5. Using a different color yarn, make a twisted cord about 24 inches (61 cm) long and thread it through the holes at the top of the bag. You can add pompoms to the ends of the cord.

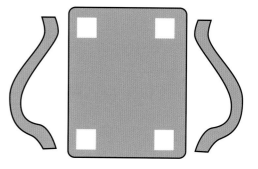

Picking Up Stitches

Sometimes you'll need to make stitches along the edge of a piece of knitting. This is called "picking up" stitches. We'll look at how to pick up stitches along a garter stitch (knit every row) edge and stockinette stitch (knit one row, purl one row) edge.

You'll Need:

- ● A crochet hook about the same size as the needles you use to knit your project.

- ● The piece of knitting you want to pick stitches up from.

- ● A pair of knitting needles. (Look at your pattern to see what size you need.)

To pick up stitches along the side of a garter stitch piece:

1 Hold your knitting so that the front is facing you and the side is pointing up. Stick your crochet hook through your knitting where the arrow is pointing in the illustration.

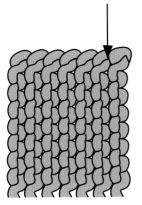

2 Wind your yarn around the hook and pull a loop through to the front.

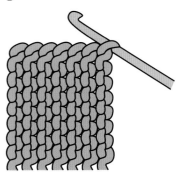

3 Keep picking up stitches this way. You should pick up *one stitch* for every *two rows* of garter stitch. (Remember, in garter stitch, one line of bumps is two rows of knitting.)

4 Once you have 5 to 10 stitches on your crochet hook, slip the stitches off the end of your crochet hook straight onto a knitting needle.

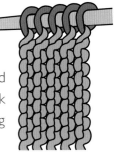

To pick up stitches along the side of a stockinette stitch piece:

1 Hold your knitting so that the front is facing you and the side is pointing up. Stick your crochet hook through your knitting where the arrow is pointing in the illustration.

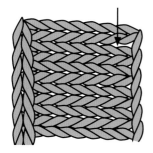

2 Wind your yarn around the hook and pull a loop through to the front.

3 Keep picking up stitches this way. You should pick up *two stitches* for every three rows of stockinette stitch. (Pick up two stitches then skip a row.) Remember, in stockinette stitch, one line of V's is one row of knitting.

4 Once you have 5 to 10 stitches on your crochet hook, slip the stitches off the end of your crochet hook straight onto a knitting needle.

Coaster

Size

5 inch (13 cm) square

Materials

- Scraps of worsted weight cotton in two colors, such as Sugar'n Cream worsted weight cotton 03 (cream) for the main color and 00042 (tea rose), 00095 (red), 00093 (soft violet), 00055 (light green), or 00028 (delft blue) for the contrast color.
- A pair of size 7 knitting needles.

Gauge

17 sts to 4 inches (10 cm) over garter st on size 7 needles.

Abbreviations

K = Knit

Sts = Stitches

Pattern

1. Using the contrast color yarn (pink), cast on 16 sts and knit 6 rows in garter st.
2. Change to the main color yarn (cream) and knit 32 rows in garter st.
3. Change back to the contrast color and knit 7 rows in garter st.
4. Bind off.
5. Pick up 17 sts along the sides of the main color and knit 6 rows in garter stitch.
6. Bind off.
7. Repeat steps 5 and 6 on the other side.

A set of coasters makes a nice house-warming gift, or team them with a matching place mat for an extra special present.

Finishing

Darn in all the loose ends on the wrong side.

Place Mat

Size

9 × 12½ inches (23 × 32 cm)

Materials

- 120 yards (110 m) of worsted weight cotton for the main color, such as Sugar'n Cream worsted weight color 03 (cream), and 50 yards (46 m) of worsted weight cotton for the contrast color, such as Sugar'n Cream worsted weight color 46 (rose pink).
- A pair of size 7 knitting needles.

Gauge

17 sts to 4 inches (10 cm) over garter st on size 7 needles.

Abbreviations

K = Knit

Sts = Stitches

Pattern

1. Using contrast color yarn (pink), cast on 50 sts and knit 6 rows in garter st.

2. Change to main color yarn (cream) and knit 70 rows in garter st.

3. Change back to contrast color and knit 7 rows in garter st.

4. Bind off.

5. Pick up 37 sts along the sides of the main color and knit 6 rows in garter st.

6. Bind off.

7. Repeat steps 5 and 6 on the other side.

Finishing

Darn in all loose ends on the wrong side.

I-Cord

An I-cord is thicker than a twisted cord (see page 53). If you have ever tried spool knitting, then you've made an I-cord—but this way is much faster. An I-cord can be used for lots of things, from purse straps, necklaces, and decorations to laces on your sneakers.

You'll Need:

- A pair of double-pointed needles. These are a little different from ordinary straight knitting needles because they have two pointy ends and come in packets of four or five. You'll only need to use two of them.
- Some yarn.

1 Cast on 4 stitches and knit one row.

2 Slide all your stitches to the other end of your needle. Your yarn is now at the end of your row instead of the beginning.

3 Keep the yarn at the back of your work and knit the next row. Pull the yarn tight on the first stitch.

4 Repeat steps 2 and 3 until your I-cord is long enough. Every few rows, hold the knitting tightly in one hand and pull down on the end of the cord to neaten it up.

5 When you've knit enough cord, cut your yarn and thread it through the stitches as you take them off the needle. Pull the thread to tighten all the stitches and darn in the ends.

Tote Bag

Size

10 × 7½ inches (25 × 19 cm)

Materials

- About 220 yards (201 m) of blue double knit weight yarn for the main color, such as Cleckheaton Country 8 ply weight in color 008 (navy), and about 110 yards (101 m) of double knit weight yarn for the contrast color, such as Jo Sharp 8 ply weight in color 506 (chestnut).
- A pair of size 6 knitting needles.
- A pair of size 6 double-pointed needles.

Gauge

22 sts to 4 inches (10 cm) over stockinette stitch on size 6 needles.

Abbreviations

Sts = Stitches

St st = Stockinette stitch

Pattern
BAG

1. Using your contrast color yarn (chestnut), cast on 40 sts and knit 12 rows garter st.

2. Change to your main color yarn (navy) and work in st st until work measures 9½ inches (24 cm) from the cast-on edge.

3. Change to your contrast color and knit 12 rows garter st.

4. Bind off.

5. Repeat steps 1 to 4 to make another one.

STRAP

6. Cast on 4 stitches using double-pointed needles and knit 40 inches (102 cm) of I-cord.

Continued on page 94.

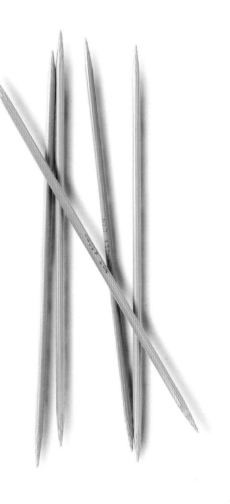

Continued from page 92.

Finishing

1. With the right sides facing each other, sew the sides and bottom together using backstitch. Turn right-side out.

2. Line up the cast-on and fastened-off edges of the I-cord with the bottom edges of the bag. Overcast to the sides.

TIP

Decorate your tote bag with puff fabric paint, or stick on felt shapes. Put a piece of plastic inside the bag so that paint or glue won't soak through to the back.

Index

About the Author

Sarah Bradberry was born in England and earned a BA in visual arts at Sydney College of the Arts in Australia. She has written and created knitting designs for *Creative Knitting* magazine. She also designs knitting kits for Margaret Peel's Fibre Supplies. She currently lives in Australia with her husband and 10-year-old daughter.